LOOKOUT

BOOKS BY JOHN STEFFLER

POETRY
An Explanation of Yellow (1981)
The Grey Islands (1985)
The Wreckage of Play (1988)
That Night We Were Ravenous (1998)
The Grey Islands (2000)
Helix: New and Selected Poems (2002)
Lookout (2010)

FICTION
The Afterlife of George Cartwright (1992)

FOR CHILDREN
Flights of Magic (illustrated by Shawn O'Hagan) (1987)

JOHN STEFFLER

LOOKOUT

POEMS

McCLELLAND & STEWART

Library and Archives Canada Cataloguing in Publication

Steffler, John, 1947–
Lookout / John Steffler.

Poems.
ISBN 978-0-7710-8267-2

I. Title.

PS8587.T346L66 2010   C811'.54   C2009-905157-5

Library of Congress Control Number: 2009935655

Typeset in Bembo by M&S, Toronto
Printed and bound in Canada

McClelland & Stewart,
a division of Penguin Random House Canada Limited,
a Penguin Random House Company
www.penguinrandomhouse.ca

2   3   4   5   6   24   23   22   21   20

Penguin
Random House
McCLELLAND & STEWART

For Susan Gillis and in memory of Dorothy Steffler

LIMESTONE BARRENS

The Role of Calcium in Evolution *[3]*
Book Rock *[4]*
Cape Norman *[5]*
Park Office *[7]*
Barrens Willow *[10]*
Wind Shadow, L'Anse aux Meadows *[11]*
Revelations *[12]*
Notes on Burnt Cape *[13]*
Location *[14]*
Warm Shallow Sea *[15]*

OUTSIDE

Dividing Island *[19]*
Marine Drive *[21]*
Body and Soul *[22]*
Under Blomidon Face *[25]*
Tree near York Harbour *[26]*
Swoop *[27]*
Inside the Boiler of the ss *Ethie* *[28]*
Beyond Names and Laws *[30]*
Wissembourg, Alsace *[31]*
Amorgos *[32]*
Sunburnt on Naxos *[33]*
There Is No One to Blame *[36]*
Bloodroot *[37]*
Mail from My Pregnant Daughter *[38]*

ONCE *[39]*

OUTSIDE

Removals   *[65]*
It *Is* a Blue Dome   *[67]*
Collecting, Bay of Islands   *[68]*
Uplands   *[71]*
Skink's Tail   *[72]*
Lean-to   *[73]*
Beating the Bounds   *[75]*
Under Mad Dog Lake   *[78]*
Battle at Halfway Point   *[79]*
Melancholy Facts   *[80]*
Bear Brains   *[83]*
Smudging the Map   *[84]*
Blomidon Head   *[85]*
In the Winter   *[86]*
After Ten Days Together   *[87]*
Without Maps   *[88]*
Kiparissia   *[90]*
Tomb of Clytemnestra   *[91]*
Mystra   *[92]*
Mycenae   *[93]*

COLONIAL BUILDING ARCHIVES

VA13 Humber Mouth   *[97]*
A10-142 Settlement at Mount Moriah   *[98]*
A10-150 Holloway: John's Beach   *[99]*
A20-86 Postcard: Cement Plant, 1955   *[100]*
A30-160 Building the Paper Mill   *[101]*
VA28 Postcard: Paper Machine   *[102]*
A30-158 Wood Supply   *[104]*
A30-161 Mill Manager's House, Corner Brook   *[105]*
B10-38 Lee Wulff Fishing the Upper Humber   *[107]*
B10-39 Lee Wulff Fishing the Upper Humber   *[108]*
B10-40 Exploits River   *[109]*
B10-43 Self-portrait, Serpentine Valley   *[110]*

Acknowledgements   *[111]*

LIMESTONE BARRENS

THE ROLE OF CALCIUM IN EVOLUTION

Sweet calcium we found we could live with,
stir into our cells' hubbub, tinker into
a trellis to carry our fierce red vine – its
eyeball blossoms, cunt orchids, cock orchids –
we could whittle it into bone stilts and paddles,
hooks, tongs, helmets, mallets, cleavers, awls,
flutes, rasps, rattles, corsets, folding spokes,
but then, oh god the weight of all these
contraptions! Just throw them out and be
light! While the old hardware clatters
down like Victorian claw-foot settees
settling in scrap heaps – the ear trumpets,
the spurs compressed in archaeological
files – we float careless as fruit flies
in an armoury, all the weight lifted,
tra-la! But the dark rock candy of history
dissolves in the rain, leaking the diatom's binary
code, the lobster's molecular gospel into
the water we drink. Sleepless we pore over
Things You Can Make with Calcium in cellular
Braille. As soon as you throw something away
you need the damn thing! Hinged pincers
down here somewhere under the catapults and
greaves. Tell me how else to deal with the world!

BOOK ROCK

If all the used cooled blood gathered
in thick pools and became rock, organic
iron ore, and we mined it to forge steel,
    then girders and rolled plate would
buzz dense with anecdote as limestone
walls – warm stone, bonestone – inside,
a humming saunter still carrying on

Cape Norman

Past the last house the gravel track widens to the horizon,

and seeing better and better,
you negotiate the innumerable stones'
deepening textures – the wheel ruts' buttes and wadis
leading the eye down a long maze – until stopped
by the lighthouse,

                 sea's plunge and assault,
gannet-owned – the beacon's rolling blink,
the giant repeated groan a conceptual monument
declaring our nation's response to the place:
a seizure
mechanically enacted for us all.

At the mist-blown cliff you scramble down tumbled blocks
once bone –
                 prehuman Egypt,
gods' jaws, twenty-ton lintels, upended stairs.

Blue shell ceramic flakes in thin drifts, salt-jewellery
fragments sharp on the palms.

In a crevice, a tuft of white grass-hairs, bobbing –
pocked foreheads, worm script on the gods' grey chins.

Daily for five hundred million years *The Paleozoic Times*
was delivered here – vast page laid upon page, accidents,

killings, jackpots, plagues, fused and fractured – you
crawl on the lost familiar text,
nylon hood flapping your ear.

Park Office

They've given me a video of Burnt Cape's miniature flowers to watch on the TV in the common room, and floor space in one of their small offices to spread out my sleeping pad for the night. The campsites are full, but the park is tranquil. Only hard-core bird- or whale-watchers or people with strong needs to see icebergs or faint Viking ruins normally come to this out-of-the-way place. Their celebrations are quiet. After Lyle and Lester have made their rounds of the campground, they hang out in the kitchen. Gordon, the park warden, comes out of his adjoining office, and I switch off the lecture on Fernald's Braya and join them.

As they say over and over, they don't drink while on duty; so they pace around, opening the fridge and cupboards, talking, pouring coffee, frying pork chops and potatoes. Gordon, paunchy, worn and rumpled, with large-lensed glasses, seems burdened by details but is willing to operate in a spirit of play. He smokes at an open window, and Lyle, shaking the frying pan on a burner, tells Gordon he ought to have his head one metre outside the window as this is a smoke-free government workplace. Gordon says he's only trying to keep from passing out from the smoke Lyle's making at the stove.

After his cigarette, Gordon goes into his office and comes out with handfuls of odd fossils and knobs of rock that he strews on the table. "No one can tell me what these are," he says. "Well, I can tell you what that one *looks* like," Lyle says. "A petrified monkey dick." "How do you know what a monkey dick looks like?" Lester asks. Lyle says he saw lots of them at the Toronto Zoo. "They're always sticking out," he says. He imitates a monkey, head held high, awkwardly walking on two legs. He nods to each of us courteously. "They're minding their own business, strolling around, then whoever's nearest to them – Uhn! Uhn! Uhn!" He grabs an invisible rump, pumps his pelvis up and down, then continues his waddling promenade, nodding serenely to all. "To them it's like shaking hands," he says.

The monkey imitation is only an exaggeration of how Lyle normally moves. His rangy limbs are always stretching and scrambling, his round brush-cut head bobbing and swivelling from side to side. He's younger than Gordon and Lester, and his short blond hair, smooth skin and gabby hyperactivity make him seem like an overgrown eight-year-old. He rolls his eyes, sucks in his chin. "If I stopped to think what I was going to say, I wouldn't say anything! An old American guy pulled over a couple days ago, asked me questions and stuff and says, 'There aren't many people smoking fish around here,' and I say, 'No, they're too hard to roll.' He reached behind the seat and pulled out a nearly full bottle of Captain Morgan. Handed it to me through the car window."

"Gifts," Lester says, "I get gifts you wouldn't believe. Women inviting me back to their tents." "Yaa," Lyle says, "they just want you to light their fires." "I light their fires all right," Lester says, smoothing the sleeves of his brown ranger's shirt. He peers at himself in the window, runs a pocket comb through his short wavy hair. Lester likes to argue, set other people straight. The Americans, he says, never landed on the moon. They staged it on TV to look better than the Russians. A bit of dirt, bit of poison is good, keeps your resistance up. Should give people with colitis a capsule of pig stomach worms. Around midnight he starts frying chopped onions, then takes two quart bottles of moose meat from the cupboard and adds them to the pan. He always gets his moose, he says. He talks about skinning them – taking the "cape," "caping" them – and the knife he uses, a fish-filleting knife shortened down. "Your best knife is a ten-dollar knife. You don't need big expensive this and that."

None of these men has any doubt about what their job is here. They're guarding a portion of nature, not from the predations of the human world but as a lure for human attention. They discuss numbers of visitors, revenues, expenses and trickle-down spending. "Down to Wiltondale in the hospitality homes," Lyle says, "they lie and tell people we're closed up here so they'll stay and spend their money right there. Oh, they'd cut your throat!" For them the interest of strangers is a nutrient their area needs. But their work in attracting this life-giving substance is strangely subtle and counterintuitive. Seclusion, remoteness, smallness, bareness and rarity are all they're allowed to advertise. If they give me shelter and show me videos of Dwarf Hawk's Beard in bloom and I spread word of its beauty, others might come here to see for themselves, or at least add this place to their known world, their owned world – a place to be cared for – so attention will flow this way and the thin local human community will survive, all because of a few miniature plants crouching in the gravel barrens of Burnt Cape.

Barrens Willow

Dumb giant, I have no words to fit what I find on Burnt
Cape: joints of a sprawled octopus-sized tree, its roots, or
are they branches, meshed with a moss-clump meshed
with a shrunken alder, or is it bearberry, sharing various leaves.

What looks like a driftwood stick – white, gnarled: I reach
to touch – is hard as a porcelain handle bolted down, bone
beads stuccoed into the somehow live grain.

Leaf-puddle tree flush with the gravel it grows in – is
the willow something the great gull of winter shat
from the sky?

Unnatural snake twisting up from a cold cleft into sun,
opening a mouthful of leaves.

It follows philosophy rather than habit, adopting any form
to suit its needs: trunk prone or upright, limbs fountaining
or burrowing.

Everything wants first of all something to hook to –
a father's songs, a sedum stem to catch a windblown seagull's
breast feather. A larch needle halts in the feather's lea. Lichen
crumbs, moss dander sift in. A willow seed opens
a trunk of its mother's letters.

Wind Shadow, L'Anse aux Meadows

Wind off the Strait of Belle Isle rakes
the cape clean. Anything wanting to live here
finds it enjoys crouching in a still pocket
behind a rock (eight months of the year
a white drift) where once in a while a companion
will tumble in: an ant's leg or cinquefoil leaf.
Just arrived is a scuffed mountain avens seed,
which in the next rain might burst its seams and
help pack the small summer room with green, except
for the week in July when it will parody snow.

Leif Eriksson dropped the erratic fact
of his briefly inhabited outpost here,
and now the fascination of tourists gusts
over the ancient site, their exclamations
and money tumble into the shadow it casts
along Route 436, feeding a clump
of restaurants, gift shops, B&Bs, new
bright-painted homes. The local people want
more boulders like L'Anse aux Meadows, more
nooks where money drifts in, especially now
that the Strait is raked clean of cod.

REVELATIONS

Envisioning his New Jerusalem rising gem-bucklered above
the aftermath trash of history's parade – the old mummers,
Rahab, Satan, Leviathan, expunged in a puff of moths and
pulverized pasteboard – John of Patmos, using past tense
for future to reflect his absolute knowledge and privileged
standpoint in time, describes how eternally solid his city
will be, adding: "and the sea was no more," showing
he counted it among the doomed forces of chaos – a waste
upon which no temple could ever be built, where the dead
could not be buried and found again.

He was wrong.
The sea is the god of accountants, though it looks and smells
like a world-sized yellow-eyed bear. As though Attila, after
razing each market town at the head of his sword-swirling
riders – driving a bow wave of heads, cabbages, hens,
painted bowls – were to pass the night in his candle-lit tent
listing in ledgers all of the day's dead, the crushed violins,
burnt shirts, hairs on severed arms. The sea has saved even
the toenails of its swallowed krill. It gathers the earth's broad
fabric falling in folds and presses it into the stone that ignorant
and ungrateful John of Patmos imagined using to build his city.

Notes on Burnt Cape

Frost causes rock to boil – wedging ice into cracks, it
splits stones, then slips its water blades deeper in,
levers them, spades the gravel up in rolling domes.

On the scraped-bare cape each strewn boulder has a wind
shadow (pointing southeast) – a tapered green plant-woven
satchel stuffed with silt.

Trees, spilt like puzzle pieces, grow their branches
down among stones as though into air, and you
must lie down to distinguish the crowns of the willows
and birch.

Sky and sea vault away beyond reckoning – your car,
the road you followed, your house, you have to work
to recall.

Sometimes caught in the wind's cold pelt, pure
sounds – waves' leisurely slosh or thump, gulls'
high slow staccato – brush past the ear
like ocean's barbed seeds.

LOCATION

I had a house here somewhere, one
concrete cornerpost poured I thought
on this lichen-covered –

                    these ants

flowing down into shadow
in a grizzled cleft, a tuft
of moss campion shrill green
while the sun fingers it, god

what time is it? I won't
get back before dark. Did I
park the car down here or up

by the road? The sea
slams and slams

and slams and slams and slams
and slams and slams

and slams its iron
door. Best to be very small,
no clothes to get caught on things

WARM SHALLOW SEA

I am sifting down through shafts of light,
krill clouds glittering in the currents,
my smoothness, my hardness, my shield I have
dropped, opened my hand and let my money
fall, I am all smile, it is possible to be only
an open door, the whole sea running harmlessly,
genially through your eye holes, ear holes,
mouth, while the shield sinks down
and down, glinting, a turning silver
flake joining the deep litter, we can stretch
completely out in the long descent, pillowed
in glow, in the water's mouth, in the sweet
yellow intricate feathered moan

OUTSIDE

DIVIDING ISLAND

When they came to the island,
she was pregnant, walked with him
slow, serene each afternoon
down East Valley for raisin pie
at the Seven Seas, lay on a lawn chair
in the empty living room reading.
Then they were three.
He had bargained to keep her
with his work, left his boy self
back in Toronto, laid out a dream
and would make a family, then
they were four, busy around
themselves, noise of themselves,
leaves unfolding, but shivered
to look beyond, greys and blacks
arranged into landscape,
snow in June, in October, proud
of their isolation, the hard
fisherman's history they'd borrowed,
but hating their dislocated selves,
their forced selves, longing to get
back to farmland, cities, unable
to give themselves to the island,
but giving themselves all the same,
keeping shrines to themselves, self-
effigies in the air above them while
they walked muddy Church Street
to the post office, watched their neighbour

chop down the roadside trees
for fuel, grief like a new seed
inside their happiness waiting
its turn, the building, then
the building's emptiness,
the scattering, that to be lived
through too, ache of a landscape
people have always had to leave,
divided from one another to grow,
to get work, hating the newness
where they went, the small picking
insistence of home, homesick,
homeless, the island growing this
history of loss like its low trees,
self-cancelling thoughts, love,
don't love, am, am not, everything
breaking down here, many small
separate parts with wind ruffling
their edges, people split and
split and finally unable to be
anything but the place, speaking
the place, if not joyously
at least beyond care

Marine Drive

The millside road, woodsmoke and sulphur replacing
air. Steam spray over the windshield. Past the main
gate, the guard booth, the yard stacked with twenty-
foot-high pulp-log rows. A log truck ahead
pulling in – diesel, spruce sap. The funnel so much
of Newfoundland pours through. Forest drawn into
this chewing mouth, comes out in paper, smoke, sludge,
paycheques, houses, lovers, mittens, photos, classrooms,
crackups, breakups, poems, single men sitting in cars.

BODY AND SOUL

Doghouse

Come back to my body,
soul, don't
flicker around
like a swallow outside
a tower window, get
in here and use the room, it's
furnished with everything
you could want.

Body and Soul Reunited

Listen, it says here
the successful performance of metabolism
is identical with the will to live.

Let's see if there are more useful tips . . .
hmm . . . hmm . . .

Saturday Night

Can I speak to a medical specialist,
please, without involving
the police?

Doctor, just put me to sleep
and keep me breathing.

Am I supposed to be singing?

I'm just being modest.
I know I'm singing.

American Hit Parade

Having a cock is bad.
Having a cunt is bad.

Having a cock is sexy.
Having a cunt is sexy.

It's bad to be sexy.
It's sexy to be bad.

The young are sexy.
It's sexy to be young.

If I'm bad I'll get fired.
Maybe if I get fired I'll be
sexy. Maybe I'll be young.

Opera

Fight, my body, fight!
Fight, my body, fight! Oh,

my visored cohort,
although your heart is a mystery,

I have always trusted you would be at my side
swinging your cutlass.

Stay! Stay!
Nothing is ever going to go wrong!

UNDER BLOMIDON FACE

spill of peridotite blocks
stalled here, frost-rounded among deepening
moss – I rest on one, its yellow baked crust corundum-
studded, snagging my jeans,
my palm's skin

scuffed sea a mile below

beside me a dwarf larch, intense green
tufts of emerging needles squint this way and that
from each twig, all up its trunk, it floats
in May light, arms and eyes too
thin to cast shadows

all my life I have lied

now wish
the air's movement, variable, pausing, lifting my page,
would fill every corner in me

TREE NEAR YORK HARBOUR

If I said the tree (a crouched
growl, guarding an armload
of charcoal) growing in Dave
Bennett's front yard, last
house west out of York Harbour,
sprouts blue vinyl quills
that Dave habitually trims
with a chainsaw, that
would be as true as anything
I can set down. You will
have to go there yourself.

SWOOP

On Blomidon face I wedge my back
in a crevice to rest. Drawn to the high
rock's rust and strew, its cloud-pocket
scrub — away from the streets
ticking with weekend errands, away
from the bottomless silence of my house.
Below, out toward Wood Island, dark
blue half-mile-long ruffles fan
across the bay. Water scuffs
over scuffs, tracks of those winds jostling
me aside. Loud on the
way down. Rowdy. Swooping.
Chasing. Their intentions foreign. Yet
not foreign. I can't pretend they are.

Inside the Boiler of the ss *Ethie*

Powdered fire blazed on my hands and jacket, brighter than the
    cloudy light should have allowed late in the afternoon –
cold fire of rust from the giant boiler,
all that was left of the wrecked ship at the foot of the cobble beach,
burning in salt water.

Irresistible theatre – human meets ocean, a slow slow tragedy,
    metallurgical *Lear.*
We darted into the fallen head of the statue of Reason, crouched
    listening to God tasting, handling, absorbing,
then squeezed out through the heavy-framed oval hole in the
    boiler's side and sat astride it –
our jeans swiped with orange –
twisting our bodies sideways, scrambling in the failing late October
    light to take photos of the iron contraptions built on the
    boiler's flanks,
carved down now by the sea into gnomic figurines, inexplicable
    implements, droll, pure. Pitted, scooped, licked thin.
The engineer had pushed his theorem out into its hardest armour,
    and the sea had mulled it, revised it into something no human
    could make,
could have the genius to make.

I had been on that beach of spectacular stones many times,
but never with her,
and the tide had never been so far out.
I had come on stepping stones before, clung briefly to the boiler's
    face and peered inside – vast cake tin penetrated by tubes –

but she scrambled into it without a word.
What could I do but follow, hands on the lace of disproved steel?

Hull deck masts stacks railings, gone, stairs cabins portals bunks
spoons, gone, but the boiler still there that had held the heat
and pressure.

We are in it, hunched in the ochre space on the rows of corroded
pipes, the place of fire, of hard waves, dark sloshing below.
The pressure, the strange stretching in our skin pulls our eyes
oddly apart.

The sea rising, jostling.

Night retracts the coast blurred in drizzle most of the day, empty of
tourists.
She swirls over and through the dried-blood-coated ducts and
apertures, untiring,
oblique,
growing invisible.

BEYOND NAMES AND LAWS

On Jackson Island Jim snared a rabbit,
skinned it, and worked a half-pound hook
up through its bare muscled ass, its rib cage
and throat, until the barbed tip lodged
in back of its eyes, then tied the hook to a line
as thick as Huck's thumb and let it trail
in the river's pull all night from their raft
moored among willow boughs,
                              and in the morning
hauled what he first took for a sunk stump,
its streaming roots the snaky beard of the biggest
catfish they'd ever seen. It was dead on the line.
They couldn't lift it. They would have towed the monster
to town and sold it and been talked about for years,
if they hadn't been on the run. Made one white
notch in its mossy back, enough for their morning
meal, then cut the line to let the dark
thing roll on ahead of them.

WISSEMBOURG, ALSACE

Despite genes and upbringing,
in the battle of digestions
I lose disastrously.

She eats the pork hock,
skin, fat and all,
all the sauerkraut,
the boiled potatoes with parsley –
only the picked bone
finally loose on her plate,
her revved-up eyes and pronouncements
ranging the room, stabbing
that and that – while my stomach
sinks under leaden
ancestral freight.
                    "Madame
has a keener appetite
than monsieur," the restaurant woman
with sparse coppery hair
observes as she clears my place.

I groan all night
in a chamber far down a shaft, down
a tunnel, deep under the Canadian Stefflers'
capital, Kitchener-Waterloo.

AMORGOS

The way my shadow jolts down the causeway ahead
of me under the street lights – crickets luxurious
in the hot night, in the tough dust-abused shrubs,
the harbour swaying in bright molten vinyls –
tells me I'm drunk. Stick man alone. Talked
for a while with a big-mustached café owner who
was born in Paleokastro on Crete, mentioned
Vai and Sitia, the palm grove, the tourist
bungalows now, as though I'm an old testosterone
lord myself, such shit, even in beauty's beauty
it's possible not to know one word in the language
of sea smell, the language of evening over an
island port, the world made of ripe fruit colours,
petting and aroused sighs, and it's possible
to be lumbering, lead-booted, mute, while
everyone else sees a living mirror that,
when they touch it, has a hand reaching from
inside, belonging to someone who is them and not
them. Place-embraced, wanted, gathered in.

SUNBURNT ON NAXOS

The grey moth probably explodes
in ecstasy, convinced it has taken red liquid wings
that light up the night.

It always saw itself fiery, expansive.

And as I fed myself to the Naxian sun on the beach at Maragas,
I thought I was filling my veins with golden blood.

Helios the butcher was making me into chorizo from the ankles up.
Slice through my swollen right shin: a pudding of fat gobs, garlic,
    maroon meat.

And I knew the dangers beforehand.
Klaus's words, "The ozone is 30 per cent reduced," buzzed in my brain
    while it fluttered into the brilliance.

The other time my skin put on a show like this was after eating
    ocean perch.
I lay in hospital three days, a man-shaped movie screen showing
    Gone with the Wind, Atlanta burning, sunsets, burgundy lusts, and
    the rash shrank into red lines all over my body like Arabic
    writing, most likely blasphemous.
I was lucky not to have been in a ward with Muslim zealots.

I am brindled again,
maculate.

Maybe the moth saw the flame as a doorway to the realm of correct
relations in which its wings are brighter than any butterfly's.

What does my maroon right ankle tell me?
That the gods have a sweet tooth. Adoration is sweet.
If, lying rapt in adoration, you should chance to attract the god's
attention, look out.

I am hobbled. Alone.
Is there no one to soothe me with cream? A woman's intelligent
hands?

There was brilliance of so many kinds. This is probably how God
punished the elders who spied on Susanna bathing.
How could I tear myself away?

The naked German girl on my right, the Polish girl on the sand two
strides above me –
her white white totally white skin –
she couldn't lie still,
was into the water and out again dripping, spreading her towel,
she sighed, her arched front meeting the sun halfway, she fizzed, she

twined, oh

oh oh the pubic down fluffed in the breeze – burning in extreme bliss
I had to lie on my stomach for modesty's sake.

In a nimbus. My body a sentient cloud of gold dust co-extensive with
the air.

Why should I be ashamed of my injuries?
It felt good, Doctor Apollo twirling his platinum needles between
   each cell.

But at supper in Klaus and Marlene's garden, lamps in the bougain-
   villea's boughs, my spoiled skin is ridiculous.
Like a silly thing I threw myself at immortal beauty and was given
   the clap.
I wrap my howling ankle in napkins soaked with beer, my thirst all
   on the surface now.

Klaus, here is the club-footed poem I promised you.

Mistakes are most interesting objects, covered with coupling holes.
Maybe sockets for new wings.

There Is No One to Blame

Where will the study of history take you?

The winter branches of the birch
are so clearly veins reaching finer and finer capillaries
into the sky,
so clearly meant to draw something
in from the light, something
down its white curving throat
into the earth.

It waits,

jostles and springs a bit in the wind.

BLOODROOT

First up through the forest's litter,
wrapped in its thick-veined leaf
against brutal April, the bloodroot
unfolds four white blue-threaded
petals around four smaller petals
around an acetylene flare.
Sun rouser. Sun's equal
in a conversation where size
is meaningless. It reminds its pale
friend of the brilliant life they enjoyed
last year. The sun would die back
to its own root if sparks from the bloodroot's
blaze did not ignite it again.

MAIL FROM MY PREGNANT DAUGHTER

An envelope with your rounded printing. I take out
a card of Henri Rousseau's *Child with Doll* –
the stocky worried girl in a red dress, clutching
a worried doll, listening, knowing the whole
landscape is going to erupt through her, life
will depend on her –

                  then your twelve-week
ultrasound with its five night-blue images
framed in calibrations and ID.
I have albums tracing your quick expressions back
to your infancy, but here I'm looking at moonlight
falling into an excavated grave. Or is it
a distant galaxy? The small gathering bones
glow where faint light picks them out,
a constellation of vertebrae. Hubble
portrait. Reverse grave.

                What a woman holds –
river of earth from the Milky Way, where we hatch,
to which we return. From my unwinding whorl I'm looking
through your night sky at forming stars.
Inside those I can almost see smaller stars.

ONCE

•

Wrapped in a shawl on the loveseat, my mother smiles
to herself awhile, then glances across with something
important to share, and for the third time
this morning tells the story of her fear of starving
when the car's axle broke on a lonely country road.
"I cried and cried," she says, still half embarrassed
by her theatrics. "I thought we'd be stuck for days,
and my father got so mad at me."
                                        "Can't blame him,"
my father remarks from the other couch.
She gives an amused snort, jauntily folding
her sweater's frayed cuffs, and follows her story
beyond where it's gone before. Her father's parents
lived in Tavistock. That's where they were headed.
Her grandfather, Adam, who'd emigrated from Germany,
was an angry, miserable man. "Oh, he hated
us," she says, her eyes live as flame.

•

The neighbour's lawn mower roars and recedes.
My mother sleeps on the loveseat, my father
on the couch. I shake out mats on the blinding
porch, gather grey tea towels for the laundry.
My father bustles stiffly out to plug in
the kettle, comes up from the cellar with chunks
of maple, measuring, figuring – how to make
wooden nuts and bolts – then is suddenly
sunk in an armchair, open-mouthed asleep,
while June sunlight storms through the house.

•

Along with the recent past, the worries
and duties that kept her fixing and pleasing
are gone. Calmly she orders him to open
the curtains, find her slippers, fetch
her a small dish of strawberry ice cream.
He jokes that he has to serve her smartly
these days, and she answers flatly that she's
done a lot of serving over the years. Without
apology she indulges her pleasures, and he
is doting and patient, almost equally changed.

•

Once, my dad's car broke down away out
in the middle of nowhere, and I cried and
cried, I thought we were going to starve!

This evening they start a letter to my sister. He says
he can never think of what to say, and she takes up the task
as naturally as she always has. Installed at the dining room table
with a pen and box of her blue-trimmed paper, silent and glad,
she easily fills a page with news – then tries to read out her words
while he waits with his hands on the keys of the new computer.

"'We still . . . have . . . a . . . a fire . . . in the . . . or . . . ov . . . evening.'"
"The what?"
"'Evening.' We did, didn't we, last night?"
"No. It was boiling hot out."
"Oh."
"Is that a period after 'evening'?"
"I don't know. Should it be?"
"What words come next?"
"Umm. 'The dry . . . sunflowers . . . are . . . covered in . . . chick . . .
     chickadees.'"
"In what?"
"'In chickadees' . . . I guess."
"Should I type 'I guess'?"
"I don't know."

•

Watching me cut a pineapple, my father says
there's lots of cans of that in the cellar I should use.

Swimming across murky Mason jars, grey
cans of salmon and split pea soup, the flashlight
picks out a stack of tins with faded pineapple labels.

I dust one off in the kitchen. The opener's
bite lets out a spurt of metallic gas.

"Throw it all out," my father says glumly.
"Everything that's no good."

•

Packed-in notes and booklets make the cupboard drawer hard to
open. Hours of small clear script. Curled and spotted. Speech outlines
on cut-apart Christmas cards. *How To Be Leaders, UCW March 18
1968.* Cookbooks swollen with clippings. *Canning Safety.* Bits of
dry rubber bands. *Oba's Chocolate Cake. Hawaiian Chicken.* Copied
on slit-open envelopes. *Potato-Beet Salad, Hedford Picnic July 14 1958.*
*Funny Memories – collar starch, button hooks, party lines. Things To Be
Thankful For, UCW Nov 23 1961.*

•

Once when she was out with a couple of girls
later than usual, her father went uptown
looking for her, dragged her home and gave her
a terrible beating. But he was worse than anyone
when he was drinking. He played at the local
dances – fiddle by ear, coronet by note –
and by the time she was ten she would go with him
and play the piano. Once, there was a crowd
over at the house, and they got drinking,
and she took a few sips – she was just young –
and climbed up on the cold stove, ha! ha! ha!
lay down on the cold stove and went to sleep!
There were always boarders in the house,
some straight from Germany, and boys
chasing her around the place tormenting her.

•

Her brother danced and played hockey better than anyone
when he was young, and when he was married, his son
Jimmy was such a nice kid. He would pull my sister
all around in a little wagon. He was only twelve.
At a friend's house an eight-year-old boy picked up
a shotgun that was leaning behind a door, aimed it
at Jimmy's face, said, "Bang" and pulled the trigger.
What was a loaded gun doing behind the door?
There was never any inquiry. That's how it was
in those days. After that her brother just worked
on the bottle return at the brewery. He could
fix radios, but he never bothered with that.

•

I round up oatmeal, flour, raisins.
"Where the Sam Hill did the cookie sheet get to?" my father mutters,
crouching in front of the cupboard by the fridge.

My mother shuffles in, small and stooped in her drooping cardigan,
pauses to root through the papers and scraps of old clothes on the desk
by the window, turns back to the living room, opening the microwave
as she goes, taking a raincoat from behind the door.

Then she's back, rummaging through the rags again.
"What are you looking for?" my father asks, clattering under the sink.
"My sweater," she says, good-natured, mystified.
"The blue one?"
"Yes."
"You're wearing it," he says.

Her face is lost for a second, then recovers with a laugh, "Oh! So I am!"
Smiling, she lingers, opening and folding a cut-open undershirt.

•

Once when I was young there was a gang over playing
and dancing and I took a sip of whisky I guess it was
and climbed up on the stove and went to sleep!

•

She was in love with Edwin Thur, but he dropped her
without explanation – "There were a lot of strange
things going on at the time" – so she walked up
to him in the street and asked for the reason, and
he said his mother told him to break it off before
he had to get married like his sister. There was
talk that his mother didn't want to lose his services
as chauffeur. The woman was a widow, and Edwin
drove her everywhere in the family car. So that
left my mother without a boyfriend. Earl Bowman liked her,
but she told him straight out she just wanted to be
friends, and he accepted that and carried on as her
guardian angel. One day Earl asked if she'd like
to go for a hike with Harold Steffler, and she said,
"Sure," and from then on she and Harold went steady.
For a while he said he couldn't get married because
he was just a foundry worker without any money.

•

I ask about the empty mirror frame on the kitchen
wall. My father glances at me and away, looking
reluctant, caught. Then speaks with odd formality,
doggedly, against some current of shyness or disbelief
or sorrow or fear. He says while they were having
lunch there at the table a few weeks ago they heard
a loud bang like a gunshot close by. He looked around
and found the mirror down on the floor, its heavy glass
split up the middle. "*You* try to get that off of there,"
he points to the empty frame. A slotted hole in its back
locks the frame tight to a round-headed screw set deep
in a wall stud. I lift and slowly work it free, then press it
back into place, centred, anchored. Enclosed blank
wall. "There's no way that could have come off
by itself," he says, bare-headed under low dark cloud.

●

Before they were married, she'd be
behind the bakery counter, tipping
cakes this way and that on her left
palm, icing them with a knife, and
my father would burst through the jangling
door with his big smile and blond
shock of hair, and out from the back
room, all pincurls and twinkles,
would waltz the owners' daughter,
Melissa, who never spoke to my mother
if she could help it, never waited
on customers. "What can I do for you?"
she would coo, but he'd politely dodge
around her, saying, "Oh, nothing,
thanks," and head straight for my mother.
That would make Melissa so mad!

•

In faded coveralls and a cracked straw hat she sits on a low stool
on the sunny porch by the woodpile breaking twigs into finger-
    length bits.
My father brings her a cardboard box of small branches to work with.

Her snapped twigs, meant for fireplace kindling, stand at her knee
like a two-foot-tall grackle's nest.
My father suggests getting a plastic bag to put them in.

"No you won't!" she says, indignant. "I don't have enough plastic bags
to be using them for *this!*"
"You've got *tons* of plastic bags!" he says factually, mildly teasing.
The laundry room is now impassable because of the heaps of bags,
newspapers, rags, basins, baskets of jars.

She solemnly takes up another stick, studies it, and breaks a piece off,
and he watches awhile and turns away.

•

Her high school history teacher –
a grave, respected man – would
call them up to the front of the class
to get their assignments back. When
she made a pouty face at the low
mark she found on her paper, he
snatched it back and hit her across
the side of the head with it. She
was so shocked, she laughs and
laughs, she was so so shocked.

•

I'd be behind the counter icing a cake
and Harold would open the door with a big
smile he had such blond wavy hair and stride
right past everyone to talk with me.

•

Although she can't make sense of the clock and has no appetite,
as mealtimes approach she grows anxious and comes looking for me.
"What shall we make to eat?"

I open a can of soup, put out bread and ham, give her carrots to cut.
She works carefully with her bent hands, angling the knife, placing
carrot sticks in a dish.

"What's that?" she asks, pointing to the tomato in front of her.
"Oh yes," she nods when I tell her.

"Would you like to cut it up?"

"No." She shakes her head with certainty.

The apples on the counter always catch her eye, though she never
eats one. "Should we have apples?"
I say, "Sure," and she lifts them blissfully in their dish and places them
on the table.

This afternoon she's back in the Fiels' bakery
during the war while my father is overseas
and her mother is looking after my sister. White
loaves, cream buns and cakes fill the display case.
Mrs. Fiel is so strict all the girls quit or get fired,
but she says my mother is the best worker she's ever
had, she likes that my mother speaks German and serves
the Mennonite customers in their own tongue.
The stingy Fiels even take out their car and drive
her all the way down to London to meet my father's
train when he finally gets out of the army in '46.

That brings her straight to their first house on Billings
Avenue in Toronto where their neighbour, a Swiss
woman, warns her that she's spoiling my father.
"What was her name?" she asks. My father shrugs
and shakes his head without opening his eyes.
She imitates the neighbour's voice: "You do
too much for him! You will regret it in later years!"
My father remains inscrutable listening to this,
then opens an eye. She had a young son, he recalls,
who was picked on by other kids and would go running
home but only start crying once he got in the house.
He can still hear Mrs. What's-her-name's voice. "What *is* it,
Willie? What *is* it?" he squawks. "It came right through
the walls. 'What *is* it, Willie? What *is* it?'"

                                        Her cheeks
flushed, my mother smiles and says nothing.

•

Curled on the loveseat under a blanket
much of each day, sleeping or merely
still, her open eyes travelling the room.

She never grieves for herself, never
stands apart disowning or lamenting
the ruin, but sometimes terrors sweep
through her, weightless spinning and inner
sleets, and she sits shaking, calling out that
she's falling, and my father or I hold her
trying to save her from deep space.

•

As I leave, she hugs me and
cries like a child. I have never
seen her like this. I say I'll
be back in the early fall, and she
nods as she goes on sobbing, not
bothering to dry her face.

OUTSIDE

In clear weather the sky over Newfoundland is thinner than the mainland sky and nothing like a blue dome. Upon the bald Lewis Hills it's easy to lose faith in gravity and see the sky as a depth into which any unsecured body might fall – sinking through loose azure toward darkness and the distant machinery of stars. The whole island a brink.

Writing in his Newfoundland journal in the middle of August 1766, Joseph Banks made these observations about the Beothuks: "Their Method of Scalping to is very Different from the Canadian they not being content with the Hair but skinning the whole face at Least as far as the upper Lip. I have a scalp of this Kind which was taken from one Sam Frye a fisherman who they shot in the water as he attempted to swim off to his ship from them they Kept this Scalp a year but the features were so well Preservd that when upon a Party of them being Pursued the next summer they Dropd it it was immediately Known to be the scalp of the Identical Sam Frye who was Killd the year before."

In fact, without knowing it, when he made that entry Banks was no longer in possession of Sam Frye's scalp. He had purchased the scalp, or scalp and face, from a naval officer in St. John's in May 1766, but in early August, his affairs in disorder because of a month-long illness, he unintentionally left it behind together with various uncatalogued plants, shells and pelts in the house of Mr. Phipps in Croque when his ship was suddenly ordered to sail for Chateau Bay. Phipps, lacking Banks's unprejudiced collector's eye, was repulsed by Sam Frye's face and gave it to Meshak Cassel, a book-owning local liveyer whose descendants, becoming the dynastic schoolmasters of Croque and believing Sam's glowering countenance to be merely a cleverly crafted mask of dog hair and leather, kept the relic in a locked cupboard beside the blackboard in the village's one-room school along with a wooden Turk's scimitar and a felt-covered straw horse head, to be taken out at Christmas together with the other traditional properties and used by the pupils in enacting the Mummers' Play, Sam's scalp and face thus being worn each year for more than a hundred and eighty years by the student, turban-crowned, playing the part of the Turk, until, in 1980, most of Sam's hair gone, his blackened features as much stitched as those of an old-time hockey goalie, he was retired along with Mildred Cassel, the school's last teacher, when the Board of Education closed the school, at which point I made his acquaintance while interviewing Miss Cassel in connection with the book I was then writing called *The Grey Islands,* and she, in an act of great generosity, on our third and last meeting, not long before her death – herself unaware of the mask's true origins, as I also was until further research unfolded them – presented Sam Frye's face to me as a gift.

Many of the body's parts are detached and retained by salient features of the island's vegetation and topography: a pair of sun-warmed breasts in the flowering bunchberries beside the trail to the top of Hughes Brook Hill where the hang-gliders launch themselves over Humber Arm (none ever returns), nettle-tettered male buttocks little changed by at least six winters among wild raspberry leaves and old golden rod at the top of the hill, phalluses too numerous to count all over the island, often mistaken for mushrooms (*Leccinum scabrum, Boletus edulis*), an ear nearly invisible among scabbed ash-coloured lichen on the bouldery summit of the Lewis Hills, feet so common as to be classified as a species of plant, *Brassica pedester,* lips in the clearspill of brooks, legs in Hines Pond, Steve Pinsent's shins in the tuckamore above Cedar Cove and along Coppermine Brook, spiky bare twigs hung with shin-skin linguine.

It *Is* a Blue Dome

the sky here today
over the Shoppers Drug Mart parking lot
is very blue and without even the finest
nick or stain
holy holy holy
I take the radio in to A1 Electronics
to have it repaired and go to buy wine
and ice cream for supper with Martin

I am roofed in blue
and although any street that I drive on
could lead to a brink, an exit,
a crypt, I feel the short-wave light
blue on my cheekbones, every object held up,
an example of its kind, clear
and miraculous, and the streets
connect in a long-learned plan
under the blue dome, down
West street to Main to the bank and
back up Park to West Valley, the liquor
store at the top, and back
down to Humber Park, recitation of turns
and gear changes I would not complain about
anymore than I would complain of drawing
breath or seeing blue sky and strong sunlight
on the maples' fresh leaves this second
of July

COLLECTING, BAY OF ISLANDS

June
23   Today a calm. Thinking of Joseph Banks I fished out the
Benoit's Cove   open car window with my eyes and at once just west of
Bib Shadow   Benoit's Cove caught (1) a Bib Shadow, *Umbra fimbriata,*
which spilled from the foot of a poplar stump on uneven
ground, it had somewhat the form of a cast-aside skirt or slip,
dark indigo among dandelions and new grass, also (2) a Faun
Faun Shadow   Shadow, *Umbra variata,* occurring where an aspen tree's leaves
sifted the falling sunlight into a school of ovals, soft yellows
and greens swimming on a blistered blue clapboard wall, the
whole aggregation fading and reappearing now and then as
though frightened into some refuge by (3) *Umbra nebulosa,*
shadows of clouds cruising overhead.

My blood was up finding such varied species close together,
yet underneath I had the persistent faint sensation of being
nothing more than a rib cage, flayed eviscerated, like that of
a sheep hanging at the butcher's, the sea air, the odours of
Dismem-   buds and pollens pulled through my chest cavity by the
berment   working ribs. Perhaps with what I collect I hope to flesh
myself out, reconstruct my anatomy in a form less human,
less estranged. Or is it characteristic of the creatures I search
for to erode or digest their observers? If so, I should list my
sense of dismemberment as one of their properties.

Cobblies   Sighted also two examples of what the local people call
Cobblies, *Phantasma lascivum,* one (4), probably a Bell Sprite
[*Phantasma medusum* (S.)], flashing in the corner of my right
eye between the blue house and the road, domed and

transparent with his edges pink-tinted and a little fringed, or so it appeared in passing – whether an effect of light reflected off the waves of Humber Arm distorted in the heated air along the road or some as yet unstudied life form lacking material substance, I know not – the other (5), *Phantasma voluptum,* is in the form of an infinite series of naked female legs high-kicking above the footlights of a stage, this occurring in my imagination upon seeing a row of white birch trunks, *Betula papyrifera,* diminishing down the grassy slope to the northwest.

24 Today being also fine I was at the mouth of Blomidon
Brook early and took what I hope will prove a complete
Aquatic Faun aquatic variant of No. (2) [*Umbra salvelinalis fontinalis* (S.)], this, having mobile crescents of light in opposed pairs like wings fluttering in abundance, resided under two feet of clear estuary water on a bed of ridged sand.

In the background, car noise swelled and tapered on the road from time to time, the tires drumming hugely on the concrete bridge, and in the intervals when stillness gathered to a heaviness that had to drop, a white-throated sparrow would sing very loud nearby, all of Earth's gravity in its words – so good to have weight, to be drawn in.

26 Yesterday and today low concourse of cloud obscuring the
Geological tops of the Blomidons, no doubt the rock outcrops and
truancy shrubby knolls are dissolved and widely dispersed in the intense mist, an absorption of elements I am convinced the rocks respond to freely, ranging far in a blind conversation of touch.

Rain Loose herds of rain mammoths, shag-sided, the colour of
rough-hatchelled tow, blunder out of the northwest very
cold, thrash through the spruce and alder knocking branches
to either side, not a fit day for venturing out.

UPLANDS

Remember there are simultaneous
and divergent contours: the broad
rolling surface of fine-leaved,
fine-needled shrubs – spruce, alder,
rhodora, blueberry, larch – and
the rising and falling terrain hidden
below. Wading through knee-high
alder you drop into hidden clefts –
only your hat afloat on the green
swell. Skirt the deep brush – alder
and spruce. Low-growing sheep laurel
and crowberries show where to walk.

SKINK'S TAIL

Some animals pace and pace in a shiver,
their eyes never meet yours or, if they do,
look right through. What you take for their bodies
is an accidental facet of whatever they really
are – a tapping toe, a keel cutting
into our element; the animal, like an iceberg,
is conducting its affairs out of sight.

What is this landscape – Humber Arm, Mount
Saint Gregory, Weebauld Island – chasing
or rivalling or running away from?

Puzzling over its blur.

               Sometimes when Jimmy
Watson's father was thinking deeply, you could
speak to him, laugh, say rude words, and he wouldn't
notice. You shrank, you scrambled among blades
of grass over dried scrags of robin shit.

Lean-to

Five hours up Blomidon Brook valley I realize I've forgotten the tent.
Sit down for a while on a rock – well, that's all right, I'll sleep under a
spruce-bough lean-to – always wanted to do that. Then, dark falling
early because of the black clouds rolling off the overhead cliffs – and
no pot to get water in it hits me now, and Jesus! no matches either! –
you feel very small among the ambiguous stems of Labrador tea,
boletus caps and crowberries looming above you. Just the wind's
Naskapi monologue – which you don't understand a word of – the
car a whole night's walk away, bogholes, deadfalls, you can't see your
hands anymore. What did she do the last time something like this
happened, in a stairwell in her underwear locked out of a hotel
room, what was it? What was it? Newspapers she held in front of
herself and went to the woman in the underground parking booth
who called the front desk. But that won't work here. Forgot the
newspapers someone said we should bring for starting a fire – ha!
start rubbing sticks. I would if I could see my arms or – groping
dead bearded faces, loose teeth – feel some dry wood. Tomorrow,
on the way back, I will find where I left my knees, assuming I can
pick out my water-filled foot-holes from those of caribou. Would.
Had I not got turned around and around in the horns and headlights
trying to cross the river. Under the surface was quiet, even the falls
felt still, your mother and you bottling applesauce in the late summer
kitchen, smooth skin on her young arms brown from the garden sun,
beads of sweat on her upper lip, your fingers puckered black from
juice, coiled peels piled on the table, hayfield heat lolling in at the
window, with her wrist she brushes hair from her eyes – when she
was five or six she says they were driving somewhere and the car
broke down and she cried and cried, nothing but dirt road, empty

fields, terrified she would starve to death. On the phone now she asks every few minutes where I am — at home in Corner Brook, I say, and she says, Oh yes, I just have to keep that straight. Around and around in the flow. On the front steps of the old Elmira house she and her father sit in their band costumes, her teenage gaze stumbling up toward the camera like a horse that just swam ashore, Papa Bismarck on the far bank, his coronet upright on his thigh. I stay unseen under the wooden steps after they've stood and left. Rain finds its way through the cracks in a lean-to. Shivering is a whole forgotten culture, step-dance ballets, tooth-click epics long before Morse code. Slowly then the Blomidons bend down through mist to study your face. Near a faint boulder not far away is one of your boots, and by late afternoon Humber Arm reaches out shaking below your shins, your car roof a spark in the tiny bushes beside the road.

Beating the Bounds

When I was six years old, my parents,
along with other adults who'd never spoken
to me, came laughing and acting silly,
picking me up, giggling, "Now we'll show
you a house you didn't know about."
"A big house."
"A secret house you knew about all the time."
So I was frightened, seeing how serious
it was that they were so strange,
although I was probably smiling,
and they carried me and other children my age
to the river and said, "Here is the marble
floor," and put my bare legs in the fast
place between stones and it was colder
than I remembered it and the tugging of dark
cold water became my legs, the Fox Island
River became my legs – afterwards when I
was falling asleep or sometimes just walking
along, the bottom of me would be moving away
like that – and they carried me, tickling me,
singing ridiculous songs among rough
brown stones up a valley past caribou
where it was cold and held me up on top
of their palms so I faced the sky and someone
with fat fingers that smelled of sheep held
my eyes open until the cold air and white
sky burned and were too bright and my eyes
brimmed like two cuts and I felt those cuts

go right into my name and they said,
"This is the roof up here, you can't go
higher than this," and that wind and sky
were my eyes then, they were in my name,
and the people pushed me through a patch
of alders and a patch of spruce the wind
had bent, saying, "Here's a young cub
we'll take home and raise," and "Push him in front
so we won't get scratched," and my skin
was crisscrossed with cuts, so I felt
those branches, smelled the alder musk,
the sharp edge of spruce like a coast,
a burning fringe, a noise around me holding
me in and they said, "This is the west
wall of the house you live in, remember
it," and the day went on like that, they
pushed me against a cliff to the north
so I felt its jaggedness in my spine,
they sat me in black soupy peat and said,
"Here is your bed, it is nighttime," they
took me down to the sea and made me
drink it and told me that was the south
and the kitchen, "the garden," someone
laughed and gave me a capelin to eat, rubbed
scales on my face, the backs of my hands
and "Over there," they said, meaning
over the hills across the gulf, "that is not
your house and the people who live there
are strangers to you, not enemies if
you deal with them properly." "They
speak a language of farts," someone said,

"they gobble like turkeys when they fuck,"
and although my body was made of all
it had touched that day and my ears were full
of my parents' voices and the voices
of their friends, in my heart I was still
frightened and felt like a stranger among them.

UNDER MAD DOG LAKE

A young man, yolk-coloured
and naked, is curled with his knees
to his chin deep in the rock
under Mad Dog Lake.

He is brighter than lava and if
he stood up, we would see how tall
and strong he is. No roads wind
above him bearing his name,

no stories are told of when he will waken
and what will occur then – a shining stranger
come down to Benoit's Cove, gold discovered,
the birth of a town famous for people

dying in bar fights or blasting rock.
Snow covers the crowberries by Mad Dog Lake
and dissolves again, and the crowberries
shake in the blue June wind, and the young

man in his deep cell burns brighter than
Agamemnon's gold hoard. And all the area's
people love him and are very careful to
never think of him.

Battle at Halfway Point

Even after the water was wounded and lying
without a ripple, it would wait until it got
a chance, then shoot a soldier in the back.

One cove, concealed by a scrap of fog,
killed four men before the scouts found it
and burnt the covering fog. Then the troops

shot all the coastline that could do
any damage. I don't think more than five
small bays got away from Humber Arm.

MELANCHOLY FACTS

How to write notes of invitation

Notes of invitation differ from ordinary letters in the following ways:
1. More formal; 2. Wholly or partly written in the third person; 3.
Date is generally written at the bottom; 4. They are without signature.

Lunch in the woods

"Oh, Mother!" said Jack. "I want to see the woods. May we take our
lunch?"
"Yes," said Mother. "We will take our lunch. We will eat our lunch
in the woods."

The Sultan of Atlas

Let us examine the habits of the more destructive brutes that terrorize
the forests, and the expedients adopted by man in contending with
them. In pursuing this subject I shall first consider the *Lion,* that fierce
Sultan of Atlas, who roams in African wilds a veritable king, so
powerful that man alone has courage to dispute his sway.

Vineyards

Let us recall the parable of the labourers in the vineyards. I will not
attempt to read it all, but it may be briefly summed up as follows:

Betty

"Oh, Mother!" said Jack. "I am so glad. I like to eat in the woods. May I ask Betty to go with us?"

Request

Mr. Jack Hood presents his regards to Miss Betty Mason and requests the pleasure of escorting her to lunch tomorrow at noon. April 19th.

A melancholy fact

It is a melancholy fact, in human experience, that the noblest gifts which men possess are constantly prostituted to other purposes than those for which they are designed. What a snare the wonderful organism of the eye may become, when–

Acceptance

Miss Betty Mason presents her compliments to Mr. Jack Hood, and accepts with pleasure his invitation to accompany him to lunch. April 19th.

As if wind was blown into it

Having brought the animal to the table, suspended by the tail, I
killed it by chopping off its head, yet the mouth continued to open
and shut and the eyes to roll intelligently. When Betty held a stick
between the open jaws, they closed with violence; meanwhile the
headless body was crawling about on the ground. About an hour
after severing the head, Mother brought some boiling water, which
I poured over the body in a tub so as to separate the horny matter
from the flesh. The moment this was done the back heaved and
the sides puffed out as if wind were blown between the skin and the
flesh, and instantaneously the head, which lay on the ground three
or four feet from the tub, opened its mouth with a hissing sound,
let go its hold on the stick, and the part of the neck adhering to the
head expanded as if wind was blown also into it, then both body
and head lay motionless and dead. I tore out the heart, which, strange
to say, was still throbbing with life. Betty put it upon a plate, where
it kept on beating until about noon the following day.

BEAR BRAINS

These clouds piled over the gulf –
bear brains or mountains – I lean a ladder
against them,
peel off my face like a mask and try
hanging it on a brown luminous
crag,

      try pasting my lips on the movement – high
cold cogitations of wind
and vapour – to feel
                    it tumbling inside
like my blood,
to speak in its language, its non-

language,
pure refusal, blindness
to my dimension –

gorgeous immortals, I
crawl on them, their cold
beauty –
          their only mercy is
that they are real

SMUDGING THE MAP

Smell of peat bog, which is not
black or brown but sharp yellow
diluted with young horn fuzz
or inner bark of the swamp willow,
can be followed walking the laps and waterlogged
draws of the Blomidons' peridotite bluffs –
ocean's secret rock-bottom plowed
arse-up on rough North America, left
chapping, waiting for the Atlantic
to cover herself. Smell of peat
bog is a zone that requires an entry
visa, clocks to be reset, nose
to think back trying to translate,
trying to remember the smells' roots.
Underfoot textures also change.
The line between squish and crunch, between skloop
and scuff can be followed indefinitely:
squish below, boulder-clatter above.
Sharp juniper growing in gaps
in the rocks, if stepped on, opens a new
zone vertically, drowns other features
under a resinous sea. A line
falls naturally around the mist
as it browses the black water of the bay,
a moving line as the mist moves
inland, up the steep slope
of the tableland toward you, a series
of lines overlapping, a mist of lines.

BLOMIDON HEAD

In the evening, in every season and weather, Mount
Blomidon's bronze head floats over the valley
and Arm, smiling a smile that is not one
we understand – more a pleased stasis that looks
to us like a smile because in spite of cold or heat
or cloud or helicopters or prospectors' stakes or
funeral processions along Route 406 it never
changes. It looms serene black-purple, black-green
in the dark, and the houses ring its base like flickering
candles. But once when I was in its presence alone
it played a tiny piano and looked sideways at me
uncertainly to see if I enjoyed the tune. And
another time it said in a small girl's voice, "The wind
kept me awake all night. Hold my feet, please, squeeze
them hard, and my ankles." And a vole I had glimpsed
scuttling under the blueberry leaves then startled me
with a laugh that was like a snowplow's blade
shaking the road, "I have eaten cities in Azerbaijan
and Peru, you will never find their foundations,
I have crossed glaciers and slept through fires
that left nothing but black nutshells and bones."

In the Winter

In the dark and the blowing snow
I found her wandering.

From afar I thought she might be a child
braving the storm for the sake of a lost pet.

I brought her into the warmth where her voice
slowly grew until I could hear her saying

she had seen me in the drifted street, a small
broken branch, and caught me

out of the wind and thawed from my clenched
teeth my story of finding her.

After Ten Days Together

Again we've lost our bodies,
become voices to one another,
construing lips,' eyes,' hands'
expressions in the slight
roughening of breath, the held
vowels. Only, now I'm here
in Victoria where you were
a month ago, watching the sun
set through your glass doors,
the Garry oak's long boughs black
and crooked as you described them,
and you are four hours further
into the night at a pay phone
after your reading, sending
your freed voice along with the traffic
on Spring Garden Road – chunks
of the country tucked into us,
folded like batter – how
could your voice from out there
sound so familiar, sound like
here when I was not here,
and the scent of your hair
on the pillow where I sleep alone
smell somehow like home?

WITHOUT MAPS

We went up Nikis, across Kidathineon,
down Adrianou to Ermou, up along Voulis,
across Apollonia into the park and out again,
and this morning by taxi down Ermou
to Monastiraki for the last time, for now.
Train to Piraeus. Up the ship's clanking
ramp among diesel trucks. Let the route
we've taken dissolve, the ladder of crutches
and luggage we've angled toward some still
island terrace, let it collapse and be lost
like my stolen journal, let all buildings
crash, all engineering, even the narrow
stairs to the room with a cot, a window,
a radio somewhere scratching faint songs
in the dusk – the route we take alone
when we can't take any other. Like the dusty
Ifestou flea market sellers waiting with black
picture tubes, turquoise hair-dryer helmets
spread at their feet. Parts designed for some
fit that won't recur. All I want is the sea's
lather dispersing behind us. You sit across
the deck, furiously writing, hurt by how
my listening fails you. In Corner Brook
blue jays are scrawling their mating calls
on the air, the woods deep in snow, sofas
of snow bending the black spruce. The intercom
announces Paros harbour. The young Canadian
couple at the rail are bound for Santorini.

Naxos for us, I say. The stern shudders
in reverse, the mild air washing back on us tinged
with cigarettes, diesel, fresh paint the deckhand
stands on a chair to apply to the overhead steel.

KIPARISSIA

We parted at dawn in the shuttered hotel room
and I stood confronting another new life
alone, gathering my things, beginning to picture
a divergent route, my enterprise more minimal still,
sadness as common as air, yourself already
become a body of longing and loss, another
defector to the empire of what was,
which I was refusing to serve, skirting its borders,
stateless, looking for some chance home,
maybe my old one approached through a new door,
when the door opened and there you stood, clear-
edged, having been out in the day, and said
in a voice shorn of distrust and pain, "Come on,
let's go to Pylos," and I said, "Okay,"
still in my small new enterprise, stripped
and raw, alone but not alone, the choice
made, our joined lives not something
either of us could invent or throw away.

TOMB OF CLYTEMNESTRA

I watched you enter the hillside vault, stand
under the high keystone, and turn to look
at the block of daylight you had passed through.
In that helix where the dead slip out of time
you went thin as a twist of light in your blue
coat and disappeared for an indeterminate
interval, travelled somewhere the Mycenaeans
had found, and were then walking out through
the light-slab door toward me, taking on
colour, gathering a shadow again, your arms
flowing back into the swing of your sleeves,
saying, as though just waking up, "God, it's
nearly one o'clock, we're going to miss the bus."

MYSTRA

In the small nave of the church of Saint Dimitri,
light passes through calm glass hands. The floor,
the frescos have been worn nearly to sleep
by the sound of sheep-bells and birds. But in the icon,
above John the Baptist's severed head,
Christ lifts like a flame in the ferocity of his freedom,
his knowledge. Even his tunic's hem is a fringe
of ignition, the start of matter breaking into tongues.

MYCENAE

I will build a skull of thick stones
to hold the sweet brain of my people,
stones no armies will ever dislodge.
I will lay them four abreast, higher
than cypress pole ladders can reach,
and the women will go in green linen
dresses, their hair long, their rooms
painted with lilies and dolphins. Neither
they nor their children will ever know fear.
What a garden the mind can become
when death is only the wish of one's
own god, the king who sends the spring
constellations over Mount Zara's peak.

COLONIAL BUILDING ARCHIVES

VA13 HUMBER MOUTH

"These photographs were taken by one of the railroad building engineers during the laying of the track in the Bay of Islands in 1890."

Inside the box, two flaking albums,
their pages loose. Wearing white
gloves, I dig into a man's summer
more than a century old, his views
of Humber gorge showing the challenge
he overcame, the fresh rail-bed
curving out of the foreground, tight
to the canyon wall. Views I know
from the highway there. Shellbird Island.
Marble Mountain. Two men fishing
near the rapids from a punt.
In this next one, something is changing before
his eyes. He's set his tripod on the new
tracks behind Humber Mouth village
and caught the backs of the houses half
turned, loosened to smoke, looking
over their shoulders in blank surprise
at the sight of him approaching, not
from the front by boat, but out of the solid
bush with his sextant and camera and dynamite.

The twilight tones in these old photographs.
Even at midday an evening ripeness thickens
the schooner's shivered reflection and hangs
in the steep Victorian woods. Breath from those bearded
woods flows down through the settlers' lanes and fences,
seeps through their walls and clothes. Darkly
in doorsills, in plates and bedsteads it gathers, stirring
like interior smoke – a palpable sleep people
can enter. Closing their eyes, they step into actual
visits with their dead. And once or twice in a decade
a bishop or archdeacon sails in to cast prayers,
baptize, marry the parents, leaving storms in the people's
dreams that slowly subside, and written accounts
of mixed cohabitations, bastards and the physical
signs of sin, children with misaligned eyes,
twisted fingers, missing toes.

A 10–150 Holloway: John's Beach

We stop where a steep field mostly
cleared of the wiry spruce rises
up from the water and crosses

the road. Hundreds of boulders,
some sheep. The owner has barred
the way with a gate and run

a stick fence straight up the hill's
side, balanced it there like a twig
on the back of a moose who will

twitch its hide in a minute or take
a step, and you can pick up your twig
and try again or try something

else, stubble, rubble, litter,
grit – the bay's flat white
water, right now at least,

would be a good place to escape
to, waiting for fish in a boat,
looking back at the steep-roofed homes,

the pale road to Curling cutting
the hill's face. The clearings would look
smooth and green from a boat.

A20-86 Postcard: Cement Plant, 1955

"A diesel truck leaves the North Star Cement Plant at Corner Brook for a load of limestone. The quarries are a short distance from the plant."

Even the sky changed with Confederation.
In 1955 it was already modern, the same
unhaunted grey I've known since 1975, driving
the Arterial Road to the college or crossing
the Dominion's gusty parking lot. The card's
foreground is a spread of crushed stone reaching
back to the North Star plant, whose long
walls – a middle texture of grey between gravel
and cloud – occupy all the horizon. Wind
is pulling the stack's thick smoke straight
east. On the gravel field, leaping before a torn
billow of dust, the diesel truck is all eagerness,
as vehement as a toy, its massive tires banishing
the old irritants, old family troubles the driver
might have had in his head if he were home
at the breakfast table. This strong angel of metallurgy
and math – which by now has rusted to nothing
but orange stains or been melted and cast back
into new boyhood, new engine noise – bounds out
for more of the limestone mountain above Corner Brook.
We will tear everything down and be something new.
Gears and dust-swirls, lunch box, a radio station –
the rest is blank black and white. The forest,
the slow breathing afternoon light on Humber Arm
are crumpled into a tin foil ball beside the road.

Between two hills at the stream's mouth,
bulldozers are smoothing an airstrip-sized
floor. The joists and trusses raised

on its perimeter already bar out
most of the valley. From this end, the far
wall looks as though you could touch it,

but it takes eight minutes to walk there.
British money is opening jaws
that will tug off the island's whole green

pelt and chaw it down.
The people in Curling and Petries forget
what they were doing and get jobs

at the mill. The fields fill with small
houses, cars out front, kids
who squint at the rim of the hills and can't

wait to get out. A place sworn
to money without much money around
is a bleak have-not place,

and these have-nots want more
roads and lights, want out of have-not,
out of far away.

VA28 Postcard: Paper Machine

First you've got to dig chunks of iron
out of some mountain – and coal – and the machines
you need to do that have to be huge
and are made of iron and coal, so where
do you start? And you blast the iron in coke-fired
furnaces and make the steel
and pour it in long solid bars
that are then turned on unimaginable
lathes somewhere else – all
the travelling from here to there in rail cars,
the ore, coke and steel and engineered
parts, the rail cars themselves made
of steel – and the twenty-ton rollers and armatures,
dreamt up by young men with brains made
only of numbers and diagrams, get sent
to the Corner Brook mill and are set up in rows
in a room big enough to hold Governor's Island.
High windows like valves for letting in
light let in a different kind
of light, echoey, smelling of electrical
sparks, not Humber Arm light,
and this light of Pittsburgh or Stelco gleams
on the perfect steel gods of the paper
machines, the exact to one ten-thousandth-
of-an-inch twenty-ton milled steel
rollers sleeping in absolute motion.
What do such things do to the space
they lie in? You must worship them and be

ashamed of all your heart's old treasures.
You must hate your lover's body, voice,
smells and the childish desires you share.
Hate the infantile work of your own
hands. You must hate this god you now
worship who lives far away in the mysteries
of the high high factories you will never see.

Two mountains of logs stand
in the mill yard to the west
of the wharves. The logs
are sent down from the Long
Range Mountains, down Deer
Lake, down the Humber River,
up two girderwork tracks
on conveyor belts as high
as an airplane, and topple
without anyone noticing, day
and night into these piles
of trunks. It is something
to boast about to people who
live where the road hasn't yet
gone. How the physical
world can be taken apart.
The people of London are reading
their papers at breakfast now,
sheets of this island, ships
fanning out over the world,
why does it make me feel weak
and stupid to speak of this?

Sunlight on an English cottage
door with fanlight and mullioned
windows flanking it, foxgloves
reaching past the sills. An avenue
of birdsong leads us there – birch
shadows on the gravel drive
and on the windscreen of the car
the manager is getting out of.
A whiff of pipe smoke and leather
car upholstery stirs from his jacket
as he shifts his blueprint tubes
to shake our hands. We'll have to
forgive him, he's very busy getting
things in place; in a week
they'll be sailing home to England
for a month – Margaret wants
to see James settled in at school,
and his brother's coming home
from Burma where he built a railroad
through a swamp the size of Holland;
it will be nice to chat with him.
We pass the hall tree and umbrella
stand. Oh, yes, thanks. Just
some water with it. Cheers.
He looks around the room. Golf
course is coming nicely, isn't it?
Next year we'll be playing on
the first of June. It's the

simplest things, you know, that make
the difference, such as getting clear
about what causes what to happen.
His cousin spent a year heading up
the Ministry of Language in Ceylon –
completely redesigned their verbs
and prepositions – now when they try
to build a bridge, they understand
it's got to sit on something at both
ends. Nothing to it. When we've
dammed the Humber River at the gorge,
we'll build a causeway to Labrador
and run the Churchill River into
Deer Lake. Would we like to take
his photo while he walks the dog?

this was probably taken by a friend,
maybe the pilot himself dipping
a wing and turning the plane tight
in the Humber valley, using
as a visual pivot the famous American
sportsman waist-deep in the river,
his arm in mid-cast, pretending
to be unaware of the racket overhead –

a bad photo, the photographer likely
laughing behind the lens at his boozy
stunt, saying, "Smile, you crazy son of
a bitch," as he tripped the shutter,
nothing in focus, Lee Wulff's rod and
gossamer line invisible, the land
like the matted hide of a dead animal,
flat, pitched at a broken angle, dull,
unlooked-at, suggested in a slur, a
darkness, a background, a passing,
a reassuring nothing you drive through,
joking, handing the bottle around, blind
movement, the stumble up from the States,
across gulfs, continents, the stunt, the
visit –

BIO–39 LEE WULFF FISHING THE UPPER HUMBER

After Lee took the boat, I waited a while
then got the guy at the lodge to fly me down
the river toward Lee. Seeing him, waist-

deep, twisting his tiny face up
in mid-cast, I started laughing. He'd figured
I was sleeping off the rum. The pilot

dipped the right wing over Lee's head
and gunned the plane around, dumping me face
down on the window – killing myself the whole

time, trying to focus the camera. Managed
one shot – oatmeal and sunspots.
That wart on what looks like a snakeskin is Lee.

I added the caption and gave it to him framed.

B10–40 Exploits River

Heading to Buchans (nothing but short
trees), the driver talks about the bear
he once found sleeping in his back seat –
he takes a pull, passes the bottle over
his shoulder to Lee, who wipes it
with his shirt. In Chicago, Lee says,
he was seeing this woman who liked
to do it while talking to her husband
on the phone. We stop for a piss and
I take a shot of Lee and the driver's
backs as they stand beside the car
facing the river. When we're driving again,
I tell how I used to wait in the supply closet
at Rutherford's for Betty to come in
on her break, always the whole time
in the dark, hardly removing our clothes,
until this one time we got carried away,
banged our heads together, I got a nose-
bleed, turned on the light, and it wasn't
Betty, it was Mrs. Purvis, the head
of personnel. I look over and Lee's
asleep. The driver thumps the steering
wheel and says he saw a bear once come
crashing blind out of the Badger town dump,
its head stuck in a woman's corset.

B10–43 Self-portrait, Serpentine Valley

An hour from camp I stop on a rock brow
over the Serpentine valley,
scuff up the sweet musk of lichen
as I sit.

Boots, pant cuffs, the camera's glint in my hand –
whatever I see of myself
is foreign,
giant beyond my real bulk.

A cloud's shadow slides down from the Lewis Hills
over the river.

The camera at arm's length, I turn toward the sun,
look at myself in the lens,

trip the shutter, flinging my head
away.

It would be like that.

I stay in the valley. All
through it.

Go back to camp pretending
to be me.

ACKNOWLEDGEMENTS

Some of the poems in this collection first appeared in the following magazines: *The Malahat Review, Riddle Fence, Literary Review of Canada, The Fiddlehead,* and *The Windsor Review.* My thanks to the editors of those magazines.

Earlier versions of "Collecting, Bay of Islands," "A10–150 Holloway: John's Beach," "A20–86 Postcard: Cement Plant, 1955," and "VA28 Postcard: Paper Machine" were included in *Helix: New and Selected Poems,* published by Vehicule Press. These pieces reappear here as parts of the groups of poems to which they belong. I thank Vehicule Press for permission to recycle this work.

Versions of some of the poems in the "Limestone Barrens" section of this collection were originally part of The Limestone Barrens Project, an art show curated by Charlotte Jones.

I thank Heather Sangster for her editorial assistance, and Ellen Seligman and Anita Chong for their help in producing this book.

In "Removals," the passage from Joseph Banks's journal is taken from A.M. Lysaght's *Joseph Banks in Newfoundland and Labrador, 1766: his diary, manuscripts and collections.* "Battle at Halfway Point" is adapted from Henry Davenport Northrop's *Indian Horrors or, Massacres by the Red Men.* "Melancholy Facts" employs quotations from J.E. Hansford's *The Business Guide; or, Safe Methods of Business;* J.W. Buel's *Sea and Land: An Illustrated History of the Wonderful and Curious Things of Nature Existing before and since the Deluge;* and B.G. Jefferis and J.L. Nichols's *Searchlights on Health: Light on Dark Corners.*

For his careful reading of the manuscript of this collection and his many invaluable suggestions for revising and shaping it, I am deeply grateful to Don McKay.

01 14

√